The Trial of Dr Buck Ruxton

by **David Holding**

First published by
Scott Martin Productions, 2020
www.scottmartinproductions.com

First published in Great Britain in 2020 by
Scott Martin Productions
10 Chester Place,
Adlington, Chorley, PR6 9RP
lesley@scottmartinproductions.com
www.scottmartinproductions.com

Electronic version and paperback versions available for purchase on Amazon.
Copyright (c) David Holding and Scott Martin Productions.

First edition 2020.

The right of David Holding to be identified as the author of this work has been asserted by him in accordance with the Copyright, Design and Patents Act 1988.

All rights reserved. Without limiting the rights under copyright reserved above, no part of this publication may be reproduced, stored or introduced into a retrieval system, or transmitted, in any form or by any means (electronic, mechanical, photocopying, recording or otherwise), without the prior written permission of both the copyright owner and the publisher of this book. No paragraph of this publication may be reproduced, copied or transmitted save with written permission or in accordance with the provisions of the Copyright Act 1956 (as amended).

Also, by David Holding:

Murder in the Heather:
The Winter Hill Murder of 1838.

The Pendle Witch Trials of 1612.

The Dark Figure:
Crime in Victorian Bolton.

Bleak Christmas:
The Pretoria Colliery Disaster of 1910.

The Last Temptation:
The Trial of Doctor Harold Shipman.

The Trial of Dr John Bodkin Adams

All published by Scott Martin Productions, 2019, with the exception of John Bodkin Adams which was published 2020.

Buck Ruxton (1899-1936)
Courtesy of Glasgow University

'Truth will come to light; murder cannot be hid long.'

William Shakespeare (1564-1616)
The Merchant of Venice Act 1 Scene iii.

Acknowledgements

I am very grateful for the support I have received from numerous quarters in the preparation of this final work of a trilogy. In particular, I wish to record my thanks to members of the medical and legal professions and the police service for the benefit of their expertise and opinions on the issues raised by this unusual work. My thanks also go to those largely anonymous yet ever obliging staff of the various institutions and archives I have consulted in my research and preparation of this work. My gratitude loses no sincerity in its generality.

The primary source for this work has been the definitive volume, *Medico-Legal Aspects of the Ruxton Case* produced in 1937 by Professors Glaister and Brash. In addition, I consulted the *Trial Transcripts of R v Ruxton (1936)* at the National Archives, Kew. Finally, *The Ruxton Trial* in the *Notable British Trials Series 3*, edited by James H Hodge (dated 1950) provided very valuable background information.

In addition, a selection of other sources including books, legal, medical and forensic articles and media reports, have been consulted and acknowledged. I would hasten to add, that none of the above are responsible for the contents of this work, and any errors are entirely my own.

David Holding 2020

Contents

Acknowledgements 6
Introduction 9
Chapter One 17
    The Discovery of Human Remains 17
Chapter Two 22
    The Police, Medical and Forensic Investigations 22
        The Police Investigation 22
        The Newspapers 25
        The Blouse and Child's Rompers 26
        The Ruxton Household 27
        Ruxton's Personality 27
        Statement of Mrs Agnes Oxley - Charwoman 34
        Statement of Mrs Mary Hampshire - Patient 36
        The Medical Investigation 38
        Reconstructed Bodies 39
        Sex 40
        Body No 1 41
        Body No 2 42
        Stature of the Bodies 42
        Cause and Time of Death 45
        Identification of the Maggots 46
        Final Medical Summary 47
        Ruxton's Interview and Arrest 48
        The Forensic Investigation 49
Chapter Three 55
    The Trial 55

  Prosecution: Closing Speech to the Jury – Mr
  Joseph Jackson KC 63

  Defence: Closing Speech to the Jury – Mr
  Norman Birkett KC.. 64

  The Judge's Summing-Up to the Jury: Mr Justice
  Singleton 65

 The Appeal and Execution 71

Chapter Four 75

 An Overview of the Case 75

 Selected Bibliography 84

 Archive Sources... 85

Introduction

This book is the final volume in a trilogy which takes the reader into the private world of medical doctors who were in practice in England during a period from the 1920s until the turn of the 21st century. Each of these practitioners came from different backgrounds, but the one common thread linking each of them was that they all stood trial for murder. Each of these cases received widespread coverage at the time, and all have been the subject of numerous books, articles and documentaries.

This book, together with its companion works, employs an innovative approach to the subject of murder. Each work commences with background information about the subject before examining the development of the case against each of them. The work then progresses to the criminal and medical investigations, culminating in the trial itself. Each work concludes with an overview of the case which draws together all the essential strands necessary to fully appraise the case. By adopting this particular approach, the author's intention has been to take the reader on a sequential journey through each aspect of the case. In so doing, the reader becomes fully immersed from the very outset rather than remaining a 'passive observer'. By the time the trial is reached, the reader is presented with all the evidence and background information to enable them to draw their own conclusions and reach their own verdict.

This final work centres on the trial of Dr Buck Ruxton, an Indian-born general practitioner, who stood trial in 1936 for the murder of his common-law wife and his housemaid. He was subsequently found guilty, convicted and executed. This case differs from its companion works in two important respects. Firstly, unlike the cases of Harold Shipman and John

Bodkin Adams, Ruxton's victims were not his patients but members of his own household. Secondly, this case is unique in that it was the first in which innovative forensic techniques were employed to provide conclusive evidence on which to bring a prosecution against Ruxton.

Buck Ruxton was born in Bombay, India, on 21st March 1899, into a Parsee family of Indian-French descent. His original name was Bukhtyar Rustomji Ratanji Hakim, which he later abbreviated to Buck Hakim. Ruxton was a highly intelligent youth who had received a good standard of education and even as a teenager, he had set his sights on a career in medicine. He entered the University of Bombay School of Medicine graduating as a medical doctor in 1923. Following his basic training, Ruxton served with the Indian Medical Service and was deployed in Iraq. In 1925, Ruxton entered into an 'arranged' marriage with a Parsee woman but the relationship was short-lived.

In 1926, Ruxton emigrated to Britain and settled in London under the assumed name of Buck Hakim. He completed further studies in medicine at London University College Hospital till 1927 when he re-located to Edinburgh, Scotland, to prepare for the examination for Fellowship of the Royal College of Surgeons of Edinburgh. He failed the entrance examination, but the General Medical Council allowed him to practice medicine in the UK on the basis of his qualifications gained in Bombay and London. It was at this time that Ruxton once again changed his name, this time legally by deed poll to 'Buck Ruxton'. It was whilst he was studying in Edinburgh, that he formed a relationship with a 26-year old woman by the name of Isabella Van Ess, who at the time was married to a Dutchman.

However, that marriage did not last long as she soon obtained a divorce. The relationship between Ruxton and Isabella flourished and in 1928 Ruxton returned to London with Isabella and was employed as a locum GP. The following year, Isabella had her first child, a daughter named Elizabeth. The couple did not marry but lived together as Dr and Mrs Ruxton. By 1930, the family relocated to the north of England, to Lancaster, the county town of Lancashire. It was here that Ruxton set up his general practice at 2 Dalton Square.

It does appear that Ruxton made positive efforts at assimilating into the community of Lancaster and created a reputation for being a diligent and caring GP who was well-respected among his predominantly working-class patients. In 1931, the Ruxton family increased with the birth of a second daughter Diane, followed two years later in 1933 by a son William. It was at this time that the Ruxton family employed a live-in housemaid Mary Jane Rogerson, a 20-year old woman.

However, in direct contrast to his professional and public persona, Buck Ruxton was an excitable, jealous and suspicious individual, prone to outbursts of rage and paranoia. It has even been suggested that Ruxton slept with a revolver under his pillow. The couple's life together was tempestuous, with Buck frequently abusing and assaulting Isabella.

On several occasions, intervention from the police was required to calm things down. Also, on several occasions, Isabella and the children left Lancaster to stay with her sisters in Edinburgh. However, these absences were short-lived and ended with Ruxton pleading her to return to the family home.

On Saturday the 14th September 1935,

Isabella had arranged to meet her sisters in the seaside resort of Blackpool where they were on holiday, to view the annual illuminations. She drove the 25-mile journey from Lancaster in her husband's car, leaving Ruxton behind, and is believed to have left the resort on her return journey around 11:30 pm. She arrived back in Lancaster in the early hours of Sunday 15th September. It appears that Isabella's prolonged absence led Ruxton to have a jealous quarrel with her later in the day, and the quarrel escalated into violence.

On this occasion it also led to two killings. The housemaid Mary Rogerson is believed to have witnessed Ruxton's assault on his 'wife' and therefore she too had to be killed. It was later confirmed that both women had been strangled and stabbed before having their bodies dismembered. It was later established that Ruxton had placed the two bodies in the bathtub in order to cut them into manageable sections. He then wrapped them in newspapers, pillowcases and sheets.

He was observed loading several parcels into his car on the Sunday. On Tuesday 17th September Ruxton was returning from the Lake District and outside the town of Kendal, he knocked a cyclist off his bicycle at around 12:35 pm. The cyclist managed to get the car registration number and reported the incident to the local police. Kendal police then contacted their counterparts in the small village of Milnthorpe where Ruxton was stopped and questioned at around 1:00 am. He was ordered to produce his licence and insurance documents to his local police in Lancaster. When stopped, he had claimed to be returning from a business trip to Carlisle. However, some believe that it may have been a trial run or in fact, that it was the day he actually disposed of the remains of the two bodies.

On the 29th September, a tourist visiting the Dumfriesshire town of Moffat was crossing a stone bridge on the Edinburgh-Carlisle road two miles north of Moffat, at a place known as Gardenholme Linn. When looking over the bridge below she saw what seemed to be a human arm protruding from a parcel lying on the bank of a stream which ran into the River Annan. She returned to her hotel and informed her brother of the discovery and he visited the site to confirm what his sister had found.

They reported the find to the police who instigated a search of the area and ravine below the bridge. This search revealed a total of 30 parcels containing various body parts.

Once recovered, these parts were examined by John Glaister, Professor of Forensic Medicine at Glasgow University, and James Couper Brash, Professor of Anatomy at Edinburgh University. They painstakingly re-assembled the bodies and confirmed that they were of two women.

A new technique of photographic superimposition was used to match two life photographs of Isabella Ruxton and Mary Rogerson with photographs of the two skulls found with the remains, and they both matched perfectly. They also used a relatively new forensic procedure known as 'entomology' (the study of maggots) to identify the age of maggots found on the body parts and thus to provide an approximate date of death.

Once the bodies had been identified as those of the two missing women from Lancaster, Ruxton was brought in for questioning by the Lancaster police. Armed with the positive results from the 'forensic' investigation, together with their own intelligence gathered in Lancaster and Scotland,

Ruxton was formally charged with the murders of Mary Jane Rogerson on the 13th of October, and on the 5th of November, with that of his common-law wife Isabella Ruxton, and he was remanded in custody on both counts.

A key piece of evidence against Ruxton was one of the newspapers used to wrap up some of the body parts. This was a special edition of *The Sunday Graphic* dated 15th September 1935 which was only sold in the Lancaster and Morecambe areas. A thorough search of Ruxton's house revealed vast amounts of blood in various parts, including the stairs, floor carpets and bathroom.

Ruxton's trial took place at Manchester Assizes Court on the 2nd March 1936 and lasted until the 13th March. The prosecuting counsel told the jury that 'It is very probable that Mary Rogerson was a witness to the murder of Mrs Ruxton and that is why she met her death'.

He informed the jury that the bloodstains found inside the house confirmed that both murders had occurred on the landing at the top of the stairs, outside Mary Rogerson's bedroom. Down the staircase, right into the bathroom, there were trails and enormous quantities of blood.

The prosecution further suggested that when Mary went to bed, a violent quarrel took place, resulting in Ruxton strangling his wife. It was said that Mary Rogerson caught him in the act.

Over 100 witnesses were called, together with over 200 evidence exhibits. Professor Glaister presented compelling evidence that the remains were those of Isabella Ruxton and Mary.

The only witness for the defence was Ruxton himself who denied his guilt suggesting that it was purely circumstantial, and he further challenged the identification of the bodies. At the end of the trial, the jury took just over an hour to return a guilty verdict and he was sentenced to death. Ruxton appealed the sentence which was heard in London but dismissed on the 27th April 1936. Ruxton was confined to prison to await his execution which was carried out on Tuesday 12th May at Strangeways Prison, Manchester.

A few days following the execution, Ruxton's signed confession was published in *The News of the World* dated 14th October 1935. It stated: 'I killed Mrs Ruxton in a fit of temper because I thought she had been with a man. I was mad at the time. Mary Rogerson was present at the time. I had to kill her'.

The prosecution of Ruxton's murders proved to be one of the most publicised legal cases of the 1930s. It is primarily remembered for the innovative forensic techniques employed to identify the victims and link Ruxton's home to the murders. This case emphasised the crucial importance of teamwork, particularly in relation to the medical and forensic aspects of the case, together with close co-operation between the respective police forces involved in the investigation.

During the 20th century, there have been many serial crimes in which mutilation of the victims was a distinctive feature. However, the Ruxton case was unique in that it was distinguished from the other cases by the extent and character of the mutilation of the two victims involved. The removal of identifiable features led to a novel comparison of the skulls and photographic portraits of the victims which proved their identification beyond doubt.

Finally, and somewhat ironically, there is the important part played by the errors and omissions of Ruxton in building up the case against himself. In this case, we see a classic example of the failure of the perpetrator of the crimes to realise the evidential importance of the identifiable articles left with the remains. The newspapers, the blouse, the child's rompers and cotton sheets in which the remains were wrapped, all helped to trace the remains back to the scene of the crime, to 2 Dalton Square, Lancaster, and to Ruxton.

Chapter One

The Discovery of Human Remains

The case of R v Ruxton began with the macabre chance discovery of human remains in a ravine approximately two miles north of the town of Moffat in Dumfriesshire, Scotland. The Edinburgh-Carlisle road crosses an old stone bridge under which runs a stream which is a tributary of the River Annan. This location is known locally as Gardenholme Linn.

It was on the afternoon of Sunday 29th September 1935 when Miss Susan Haines Johnson, a visitor to the area from Edinburgh, crossed the bridge and gazed below into the ravine and stream. On the bank of the stream she noticed a bundle wrapped in newspaper revealing what she believed was a human arm. Shocked by what she had witnessed, she hurried back to the hotel where she was staying with her brother Alfred. On hearing Susan's report, Alfred went to the ravine himself to confirm what had occurred. Climbing down into the ravine he discovered other parcels containing human remains some wrapped in newspapers and others in a cotton sheet. Their discovery was quickly relayed to the local police at Moffat who instigated a full search of the locality.

The search revealed four bundles; together with two heads, a thigh bone (femur), two forearms with attached hands, and various pieces of human flesh and skin. The collected remains were removed to the small mortuary attached to Moffat Cemetery. On close examination, the first bundle contained two upper arms and four pieces of flesh wrapped in a blouse. The second bundle revealed two thigh-bones (femora), two legs with most of the tissue removed and pieces of flesh, enclosed in a pillowslip. The third bundle which was covered with a cotton sheet contained seventeen pieces of flesh. The fourth bundle contained the chest portion of a human trunk, together with two legs tied together with a piece of hem from a cotton sheet, and mixed inside was straw and cotton wool. Around some of the bundles and also lying on the ground were pieces of newspaper. One particular piece of newspaper was identified as part of *The Sunday Graphic and Sunday News* dated 15th September 1935, and this was found in the first bundle. Later in the investigation, this proved to be an important clue.

Each of the two heads was wrapped in cotton wool and a pair of child's rompers, held in position with a piece of cotton twine. The initial police search was resumed at Gardenholme Linn the following day, 30th September, when another forearm with hand and a piece of flesh, each wrapped in newspaper, an uncovered thigh (femur), together with another bundle containing a pelvis, were found just below the bridge on the bank of the stream.

The police continued their search around the Linn and on the 2nd October another five pieces of flesh were retrieved. It was not until the 28th October that a roadman discovered a newspaper bundle containing a left foot on the side of the Glasgow-Carlisle road nine miles south of Moffat. Finally, on 4th November 1935, a woman walking along the Moffat-Edinburgh road, half a mile south of Gardenholme Linn, discovered a forearm and hand, wrapped in newspaper, lying in the grass at the road.

In total, the police search revealed seventy pieces of human remains, including two heads and one trunk. On the morning of Monday 30th September, the day following the discovery of the remains, they were examined at the Moffat mortuary by two local general practitioners, Dr David Huskie and Dr F W Pringle.

On the following day, Tuesday 1st October, Dr W Gilbert Millar, Lecturer in Pathology at the University of Edinburgh and Professor John Glaister, Regius Professor of Forensic Medicine also at Edinburgh University first visited the scene of the discovery, followed by a preliminary examination of the remains at the Moffat mortuary.

It was soon realised that identification of the dismembered and mutilated bodies posed a difficult problem, and that reconstruction would be essential. In addition, the decomposing and maggot-ridden remains required urgent preservation. Since there were no facilities at the mortuary to accommodate this mammoth task, the remains were transported to the University at Edinburgh.

The preliminary examination of the remains at Moffat did confirm certain basic facts. They represented at least two bodies which were described as 'well-developed and well-nourished'. It was also apparent that both heads had been mutilated by the removal of the main features - ears, eyes, nose, lips and facial skin - together with teeth extracted, most probably after death.

The less-mutilated head was considered to be that of a young woman, whilst the other first appeared to be that of a man but was later acknowledged to be that of an older woman when the accompanying pelvis was attached to the remains. It was of medico-legal significance that many of the missing parts were those that could reveal marks of violence suggesting possible cause of death

The unanimous view of the experts involved in the examination of the remains, was that the person or persons responsible for the mutilation and dismemberment of the two bodies displayed both medical and anatomical knowledge. This was further reinforced by the fact that the bodies had been dismembered into neat portions convenient for their ultimate disposal. This had been carried out by cutting through the joints with a knife or possible surgical scalpel. There were no visible signs that a saw had been used in carrying out this task.

Those parts of the remains thought likely to belong to each of the bodies were stored in separate boxes labelled 'Body No 1' and 'Body No 2'. The first box contained the head and the other various component parts which initially appeared to belong to the body of a young woman. Since the investigation would involve a wide field of medico-legal expertise, the specialists involved, were assigned to specific areas of investigation.

Professor Glaister, his assistant Dr FW Martin, together with Dr Millar, were responsible for the pathological and medico-legal aspects of the case. The anatomical investigation which would include the reconstruction of the bodies, was the responsibility of Professor Brash, assisted by Dr E Llewellyn Godfrey, a specialist radiographer. The dental examination of the skulls was undertaken by Dr ACW Hutchinson, Dean of the Dental Hospital and School at Edinburgh University, assisted by A Johnstone Brown, a local dental surgeon. By combining the medico-legal investigations, various lines of inquiry could be carried out in parallel, and frequent daily discussions ensured that the work was closely co-ordinated. Photographic recordings were undertaken of all the relevant body parts in preparation for anticipated criminal proceedings. This work was undertaken by members of the City of Edinburgh Police Force. Whilst there were essentially two investigations being undertaken simultaneously, one by the medical team the other by the respective police forces, close contact between the two was maintained to provide a co-ordinated overview of the case.

2, Dalton Square, Lancaster, Ruxton's House
Commons Attribution Photo

Chapter Two

The Police, Medical and Forensic Investigations

The Police Investigation

Following the discovery of the human remains at Moffat on 29th September, 1935, the police launched their own investigation which involved pooling their resources between three separate Scottish forces - Dumfriesshire Constabulary, Glasgow Police Force and the City of Edinburgh Police Force - each contributing its own specialist officers. This was a good example of inter-force co-operation, in helping to gather as much evidence as possible to ultimately secure a conviction of the person or persons responsible for this horrific crime.

Detective Inspector John Sheed, an officer attached to Edinburgh Police, was appointed as liaison officer between the medical experts at Edinburgh University and the respective police forces. This ensured that there was co-ordination between the medical evidence and the police lines of enquiry. At this point, Dumfriesshire Constabulary (on whose territory the remains were found) was the lead force.

One of the first tasks undertaken by officers of the Dumfriesshire Police (and assisted by other officers drafted in from nearby Lanarkshire Constabulary) was to carry out further searches along the stream at Gardenholme Linn, the site of the original discovery. This included observing the positions in which the remains had been found, and it was concluded that the remains had been thrown over the bridge parapet, very likely at night, by someone who was familiar with the locality, but not with the course of the narrow stream flowing below. By observing the state of the stream banks, it was revealed that the stream had recently flooded.

Information gathered locally at Moffat confirmed that the stream had been in spate during the night of 17th/18th September, the water still being relatively high on the 19th September. From local knowledge it was confirmed that floods in the stream tended to subside relatively quickly. This information was of particular importance to the police investigation because some pieces of flesh had been located on the bank of the stream, and others on the bank of the River Annan some 600 yards further down than the bridge. It had also been noted that after 18th September, this had been followed by four or five dry fine days.

This provided a provisional time-line for when the remains had been deposited in the ravine. It was suggested that this possibly occurred about the time that the stream was flooded, on the 16th, 17th or 18th September 1935.

Local weather records showed that the heaviest rainfall at Moffat during September had been on the 18th, when nearly one and a half inches of rain had fallen. Particularly during the night between Sunday and Monday, 15th and 16th September, there had been a fairly heavy rainfall. The chief difficulty facing the police at this point in their investigation in tracing the remains was that the Moffat-Edinburgh road is a main route between England and the North.

The police issued a statement that they required information from garages and petrol stations regarding any suspicious cars or occupants having used them. The next line of enquiry was to search recent reports of missing persons. The investigators deduced that it would be very unlikely that two persons, associated in some way, could disappear within a short time-frame without at least one other person being aware of the fact. Consequently, the police concentrated their attention on reports of dual disappearances.

It also became evident to investigators that if performed by one person, even if that one person had anatomical knowledge, the extent of the mutilations and dismemberment of the bodies must have made it a considerable undertaking. Equally important was the fact that there must have been the opportunity for carrying out this work undisturbed for several hours. This suggested that the bodies of the victims had been dismembered in the same location in which they had been killed. This theory was reinforced by the fact that many of the body parts had been completely drained of blood. In addition, various 'domestic' articles had been found with the remains, for example, newspapers, cotton sheeting, child's rompers, a blouse and cotton wool.

On the 9th October, the Chief Constable of Dumfries contacted the Lancaster Borough Police because of an article he had seen in *The Glasgow Daily Record* regarding the disappearance three weeks previously of a young Lancaster woman named Mary Jane Rogerson. She had been employed as nursemaid by a local Dr Buck Ruxton who was practising in Lancaster. He was informed by Lancaster Police that the disappearance of this girl had been reported to them. It is also of significance that on 24th September, Dr Ruxton had visited the police station in Lancaster complaining that local rumours had begun to circulate regarding the discovery that the human remains discovered in Scotland were those of his wife and maid. He maintained that these rumours were proving detrimental to both his medical practice and his general reputation. On this occasion, he also told the police that his wife had left him two weeks before and gone to Scotland.

The Newspapers

As part of their continuing investigation, the police had carefully examined the wrappings in which the human remains had been found, in an attempt to discover links between them. It emerged from this examination that the latest date of any of them was the 15th September, 1935. This proved to be a vital clue because this date was when the missing women from Lancaster disappeared.

Three different newspapers were identified; *The Sunday Herald, The Sunday Chronicle* and *The Sunday Graphic and Sunday News*. Two pieces from *The Sunday Graphic and Sunday News*, proved to be of vital importance to the police investigation. One of the pieces bore the serial number 1,067, and further police enquiries revealed that the newspaper was one of 3,700 copies of a special 'slip' edition which covered the Morecambe Carnival held on Saturday 14th September. This had been issued to a few newsagents in Morecambe, Lancaster and the surrounding districts only.

Police confirmed that the copies of the issue had been supplied to a wholesale newsagent in Lancaster. He had received 728 copies on Sunday 15th September, and he, in turn, had supplied 24 copies to another retailer in Lancaster. This retailer was able to confirm that Dr Buck Ruxton was one of his customers and that every Sunday for the past twelve months, he had a copy of the paper delivered to him. On Sunday 15th September 1935, a copy of the paper was duly delivered to 2 Dalton Square by a local paper boy.

The Blouse and Child's Rompers

Following the newspaper evidence, Scottish police visited the Rogersons in Morecambe and asked Mary's parents if they could identify any of the clothing found with the human remains at Moffat. Mrs Rogerson, Mary's step-mother, immediately recognised the blouse because of the distinctive patchwork repair she had carried out under one of the arms, prior to giving it to Mary.

While Mrs Rogerson was unable to recognise the pair of child's rompers, she suggested that the police show the article to a friend of hers Mrs Edith Holme, living at Grange-over-Sands. It transpired that Isabella Ruxton, Mary and the children had stayed at Mrs Holme's earlier in 1935 while on a short holiday to Morecambe Bay.

When the rompers were shown to Mrs Holme, she immediately recognised them as a pair she had bought and given to one of the Ruxton children. She had replaced the worn elastic waist band and secured it with her own unique style of knot. With this new information, the direction of the police investigation became firmly focused on Lancaster, and on Ruxton in particular.

It was at this stage that the overall supervision of the investigation was taken over by Lancaster Borough Police, the responsibility being transferred to Captain Henry J Vann, the Chief Constable. In order to assist the reader in placing subsequent events in context, a brief background to the Ruxton household and in particular, Ruxton's personality was considered useful.

The Ruxton Household

In addition to Dr Buck Ruxton and his common-law wife Isabella, the household at 2 Dalton Square, Lancaster, comprised their three children; daughter Elizabeth aged six, daughter Diane aged four and son William aged two. The Ruxtons also employed a live-in nursemaid Mary Jane Rogerson, aged twenty. The domestic housework and cooking were shared by two charwomen. Mrs Agnes Oxley worked at the house every day of the week starting around 7:10 am, and Mrs Elizabeth Curwen also worked every day, starting at 8:30 am except Sundays when she started work at 10:00 am. Both these charwomen lived in Lancaster and were not resident at Dalton Square.

Ruxton's Personality

Since settling at Dalton Square in 1930, there was no doubt that the relationship between Ruxton and Isabella had become strained and tense. This was because of Ruxton's paranoid suspicions of Isabella's alleged infidelity, demonstrated by furious outbursts and threats made in the presence of witnesses. Previous maids employed at the house recalled his threatening attitude towards his wife, and of him having a revolver in his bedroom. They even witnessed occasions when knives had been held at Isabella's throat by Ruxton, and the police had been called on at least two occasions because of his threatening and erratic behaviour. They had described Ruxton as 'acting like a madman, becoming so excited as to be completely incoherent'.

In 1932, Mrs Nelson, one of Isabella's sisters living in Edinburgh, had travelled down to Lancaster in response to a telegram she had received from

Ruxton informing her that Isabella had attempted to commit suicide. Again in 1934, Mrs Ruxton had gone up to Edinburgh with the children to escape the increasing threats and violence. She was followed by Ruxton and persuaded to return with him to Lancaster. There was no doubt that Ruxton's jealousy and growing belief in Isabella's infidelity was that of an unbalanced person. It has been regarded by many as the overriding factor in Ruxton's final criminal act. His extreme personality disorder was clearly demonstrated in two final events which occurred within one week of each other in early September 1935.

On Saturday 7th September, Mrs Ruxton visited Edinburgh in the company of local friends, the Edmondson family, comprising Mr and Mrs Edmondson, their daughter and son Robert. The party travelled to Edinburgh in two cars, staying overnight at the Adelphi Hotel, all occupying separate rooms. Ruxton was convinced that this visit was really an illicit meeting arranged between Isabella and the young Robert Edmondson, so he hired a car and followed the party.

His suspicions were completely unfounded but this event clearly demonstrated how even an innocent trip to Scotland became completely distorted in Ruxton's mind. The following Saturday, 14th September, Mrs Ruxton arranged to meet her two sisters who had come down from Edinburgh for a break in Blackpool. Each year they met up to view the illuminations together. Isabella travelled in her husband's car alone, leaving Ruxton with Mary the housemaid at home.

It was established that Isabella left Blackpool for the twenty-five mile journey back to Lancaster at approximately 11:30 pm. She is believed to have arrived back at Dalton Square in the early hours of Sunday 15th September, because Ruxton's Hillman Minx car was seen parked outside the house on the Sunday morning. Leaving Blackpool on the Saturday night was the last time that anyone but Ruxton saw her alive. Mary Rogerson the maid was last seen at the house around 7 pm.

On Friday 13th September, one of Ruxton's charladies, Mrs Curwen, was working at the house when she was told by Ruxton that since there was nothing for her to do that day, she could go home, and only need to report for work on Monday 16th September. Then on Sunday 15th September at 6:30 am, Ruxton visited his other charlady, Mrs Oxley, who was due to start work that day at 7:10 am, and told her that she too did not need to come to work, but that she should come as normal on the Monday morning. These two incidents have been interpreted by observers of the case, as evidence that Ruxton was preparing to carry out his crime and therefore ensured that there would be no witnesses present. Various people called at Dalton Square on the Sunday and commented on the delay in opening the door by Ruxton himself, when usually this was done by either Mary Rogerson or one of the two charladies.

Those visitors who commented about Ruxton's bandaged right hand were given various explanations for the injury. Amongst the explanations were the declaration that he had 'jammed it', or that he had cut it opening a tin of fruit for his children's breakfast.

Later that Sunday morning, Ruxton had visited two garages to obtain petrol. At 11:00 am, a Mrs Whiteside called accompanied by her young son to keep an appointment for a minor operation to be performed. Ruxton opened the door and apologised that he was unable to carry out the operation that day. The reason he gave was that Mrs Ruxton was away in Scotland and there were only himself and Mary his maid present. They were busy removing carpets in preparation for decorators arriving on the Monday morning.

At about 11:30 am, Ruxton took his children over to the Andersons, family friends in Morecambe, where the children would stay for a few days. On his return from Morecambe, Ruxton was alone at his house until about 4:30 pm when he visited one of his patients, a Mrs Hampshire. He requested that she help him clean the house because he had cut his hand and was finding it difficult. He explained that his wife was in Blackpool and Mary Rogerson was away in Edinburgh.

When Mrs Hampshire arrived back at Dalton Square, she found the house in a very untidy state. Carpets had been removed from the stairs and replaced by straw, and some of these carpets lay with a blue suit in the waiting-room. In the rear yard, she found other carpets, clothing and towels all heavily blood-stained. There was evidence that an attempt had been made to burn these items.

Mrs Hampshire noted in particular that the doors to two bedrooms were locked, and that in the lounge there was a supper laid out for two. This was untouched. She was particularly surprised to find that the bath was in a very dirty state, being stained with a dirty yellow colour. Mrs Hampshire was later joined by her husband to help with the cleaning. Later that evening, Ruxton offered the carpets and suit in the waiting-room to the Hampshires even though they were stained, and they took them away when they left the house at around 9:30 pm. From that time until the morning of Monday 16th September, nothing was known of Ruxton's movements.

At about 7:00 am on the morning of Monday 16th September, Mrs Oxley had arrived at Ruxton's house as usual, but could receive no answer so she went back home before returning at about 9:15. At 9.00 Ruxton visited Mrs Hampshire again to enquire about the carpets and suit he had given her.

It is particularly significant that Mrs Hampshire recalled Ruxton looking very ill, unshaven and wearing an old raincoat, certainly not in keeping with his usual smart appearance. Picking up the suit, Ruxton asked for a pair of scissors to cut out his name from the jacket which was then thrown on the fire. He told Mrs Hampshire that if she could not clean the items, then they should be burned. When Ruxton had left, Mrs Hampshire swilled the carpet with numerous buckets of water which turned red like blood. While Mrs Oxley was standing at the front door, Ruxton arrived in his car having just left the Hampshires. In later interviews, she described Ruxton's appearance almost exactly as that described by Mrs Hampshire. When Mrs Oxley eventually entered the house, she too found the same bedroom doors locked and the uneaten supper still in the lounge. It transpired that later on the Monday, Ruxton had left his own car at his usual garage for servicing and had hired another car. Nothing is known of Ruxton's movements for the rest of the day. On Tuesday 17th September at about 1:00 pm, Ruxton was stopped in his hired car at Milnthorpe, between Kendal and Lancaster.

It appears that he had knocked down a cyclist at Kendal that afternoon and failed to stop. He told the police that he had been to Carlisle on business. On Thursday 19th September, Ruxton requested an early breakfast from his charlady, telling her that he was going to see a specialist about his injured hand. At around 7:30 am, he brought his car to the back door of his house and was heard to go up and down the stairs several times and go out to his car. At approximately 8:00 am, he left Dalton Square and did not return until about 3:30 pm saying that he had been to Blackburn.

Later that day, his three children returned from Morecambe. When Ruxton had left on the Thursday morning, the charladies noticed that the two bedroom doors were open, and that there was an offensive smell in his bedroom. On Friday 20th September, Ruxton asked one of the charladies to go and buy a spray of eau-de-cologne which he then used throughout the house.

From information received by the police from various sources, suspicion was now firmly centred on Dr Buck Ruxton. His conduct at various interviews with the police, together with their knowledge of his jealous, violent disposition and unhappy relationship with Isabella, was a sufficient basis for this suspicion. The date of *The Sunday Graphic and Sunday News* found with the remains at Moffat was the very same date on which the two women disappeared from Lancaster.

This connecting link was further strengthened by the fact that circulation of this particular edition of newspaper was restricted to the Morecambe and Lancaster areas. On the 10th, 11th and 12th October, blood-stained carpets and stair-pads from Ruxton's home, together with the blood-stained jacket and trousers were recovered from Mrs Hampshire. Also, by the 12th October, the child's rompers and blouse had been positively identified as belonging to Mary Rogerson. Later that day, Chief Constable HJ Vann of the Lancaster Borough Police Force requested Ruxton attend the police station for an interview regarding the two missing women.

The most crucial element of the evidence linking the remains at Moffat with No 2 Dalton Square, Lancaster, were the numerous imprints found on articles in the house which were identical with the fingerprints of Body No 1 (Mary Rogerson). Those prints were found all over the house including in Mary Rogerson's bedroom and on articles which the maid would handle in the course of her work.

It can be seen from Table 1 (later in the book) that in the case of Mary Rogerson, numerous imprints were positively identified, notably the fingerprints of both hands, and palmar impression of the left hand. These placed the identify of Body No 1 beyond doubt.

On 13th October 1935, Detective Lieutenant Hammond, Officer in charge of the Finger Print Department of the City of Glasgow Police, visited Ruxton's house. He spent 11 days photographing fingerprints and palm-imprints, comparing them with those of the left hand of Body No 1, together with the other impressions from the hands of nine other persons with legitimate access to the house, including those of Ruxton himself. Three palm impressions and thirty-one fingerprints were positively identified as having been made by the left hand of Body No 1.

At Ruxton's subsequent trial, Lieutenant Hammond explained to the jury the principles underlying identification by means of fingerprints and palmar impressions. He demonstrated these on enlarged photographs, the agreement between those from the house and those of the left hand of Body No 1. In order to confirm that those fingerprints from the house were made by the hand of Body No 1, he would be satisfied with 8 points of similarity, showing characteristics and agreement.

In comparing the prints from various articles with the prints taken from Body No 1, he had shown more than 8 points of agreement in each case. In the comparison of the palmar impressions on the leaf of a table with the palmar impressions of the left hand of Body No 1, he had marked 20 points of agreement on the enlargement photographs.

Some of the strongest evidence against Ruxton came from his charwomen whom the police had interviewed on several occasions. In particular, Mrs Agnes Oxley and Mrs Mary Hampshire helped the police to construct a time-line of Ruxton's movements subsequent to the disappearance of Mrs Ruxton and Mary Rogerson on Saturday 14th September, 1935. The following two extracts from statements made by both women, helped to strengthen the police case against Ruxton.

Statement of Mrs Agnes Oxley - Charwoman

Mrs Oxley was a Charwoman employed by Dr Ruxton at 2 Dalton Square, Lancaster, to undertake domestic cleaning and share cooking with another Charwoman, Mrs Elizabeth Curwen. Mrs Oxley attended the doctor's house every day, commencing work at 7:10 am and finishing her work at various times. On Sunday, 15th September, 1935, she was preparing to leave her home to arrive at Ruxton's house for her usual time. However, at 6:30 am, Ruxton made an unexpected visit and spoke to her husband. He told him to 'Tell Mrs Oxley not to trouble to come down this morning. Mrs Ruxton and Mary have gone on holiday to Edinburgh. I am taking the children to stay in Morecambe with friends. Tell her to come down as usual on Monday'.

On the morning of Monday 16th September, Mrs Oxley arrived at Ruxton's house at approximately 7:00 am. After ringing the door bell several times and getting no reply, she went back home and then returned at 9:15 am to find Ruxton arriving in his car. Mrs Oxley noted in particular the appearance of Ruxton on that occasion, being used to Ruxton being very smartly presented. On this occasion he looked ill, was unshaven, without a collar and tie, and wearing an old raincoat, completely out of character. Mrs Oxley accompanied Ruxton into the house, made him some coffee and then went into the surgery to assist him to bandage his cut hand. He explained to her that he had cut his hand trying to open a tin of fruit for the children's breakfast with a tin-opener that was bent. In the process, he had lost a lot of blood.

Mrs Oxley noticed an untouched meal laid out in the lounge. All the stair carpets had been removed and the stairs scattered with straw. Rolled-up carpets, stair pads and a man's suit were lying in the waiting-room. In the back yard, she saw other carpets, clothing and towels all heavily blood stained, and signs that attempts had been made to burn them. She particularly noticed that the doors to the doctor's bedroom, the drawing room and the dining room were all locked and no keys left in the locks. She also remarked that she had never seen a bath in such a dirty state, stained with *a yellow colour. She distinctly remembered that it was not in that state on the Saturday 14th September, because Mary Rogerson had cleaned it. She cleared away the untouched meal in the lounge, then left the house at 12:30 pm, her work complete.*

On the morning of Thursday 19th September, Ruxton asked Mrs Oxley to make breakfast quickly because he was going to see a specialist regarding his injured hand. She was working in the kitchen around 7:20 am when Ruxton brought his car to the backdoor of the house. Mrs Oxley remembered that Ruxton made several journeys between his car and the upstairs rooms. He finally left the house at 8:00 am, arriving back about 3:30 pm. When Ruxton had gone, Mrs Oxley found that the doors to the upstairs rooms which had been previously locked were now unlocked. She also noticed a foul smell coming from these rooms.

Statement of Mrs Mary Hampshire - Patient

On Sunday 15th September 1935, at approximately 4:30 pm in the afternoon, Ruxton visited the home of one of his patients, Mrs Mary Hampshire. He informed Mrs Hampshire that he was preparing the house for decorators who would be coming on Monday 16th September. He had cut his hand and required some help in preparing for them. He told Mrs Hampshire that Mrs Ruxton had gone to Blackpool and Mary Rogerson was in Edinburgh. Mrs Hampshire went back with Ruxton to the house which she found completely empty. She noticed a meal laid untouched in the lounge. Finding that there was a lot of cleaning to be done, she asked Ruxton if her husband might be asked to help and he agreed. The carpets had been removed from the stairs and landings. She saw straw scattered around and some protruding from beneath the doors of the two bedrooms occupied by Ruxton and his wife, they were both locked. Some rolled-up carpets, stair pads and a man's suit lay in the waiting-room. Ruxton asked her to clean the bath which was a dirty yellow colour which came to within six inches of the top. In the back yard Mrs Hampshire found two carpets from the landings, together with stair carpets, one badly stained with blood, together with a blood-stained shirt and partially burned blood-stained towels.

About 4:30 pm, Ruxton left to take his children to a dentist family friend in Morecambe, the Andersons. He returned later to collect the children's night clothes. He took Mr and Mrs Hampshire into the waiting-room and told them that they could take away the stair carpets and the blue suit with blood stains if they wished to have them. They finished the cleaning and dusting and left the house at 9:30 pm. On Monday 16th September at approximately 9:00 am Ruxton called again at Mrs Hampshire's home asking that she gave him back the suit so that he could get it cleaned himself. He pointed to a tab in the pocket of the suit coat which bore his name and told Mrs Hampshire to 'cut it off and burn it' which she did. She asked Ruxton where Mrs Ruxton was, and he said that she was on holiday in Edinburgh. The suit waistcoat was so blood-stained that she could do nothing with it and burned it. She then untied the bundle of carpets and found that one of them, a stair carpet, was damp with blood. She took this carpet out into her back yard and threw between 20 and 30 buckets of water over it without being able to get it clean. The water which ran off the carpet was like blood flowing away.

The Medical Investigation

Even the substantial amount of evidence already collected by the police during their investigation was insufficient to obtain a conviction against Dr Buck Ruxton. If the medical experts at Edinburgh University were unable to establish that the remains discovered at Moffat were those of Isabella Ruxton and Mary Rogerson, the case against Ruxton would collapse. The experts combined not only well-established forensic methods in their task, but also employed innovative techniques to ascribe the remains to each of the respective bodies. Initially, they were given the designation of Body No 1 and Body No 2.

Reconstructed Bodies

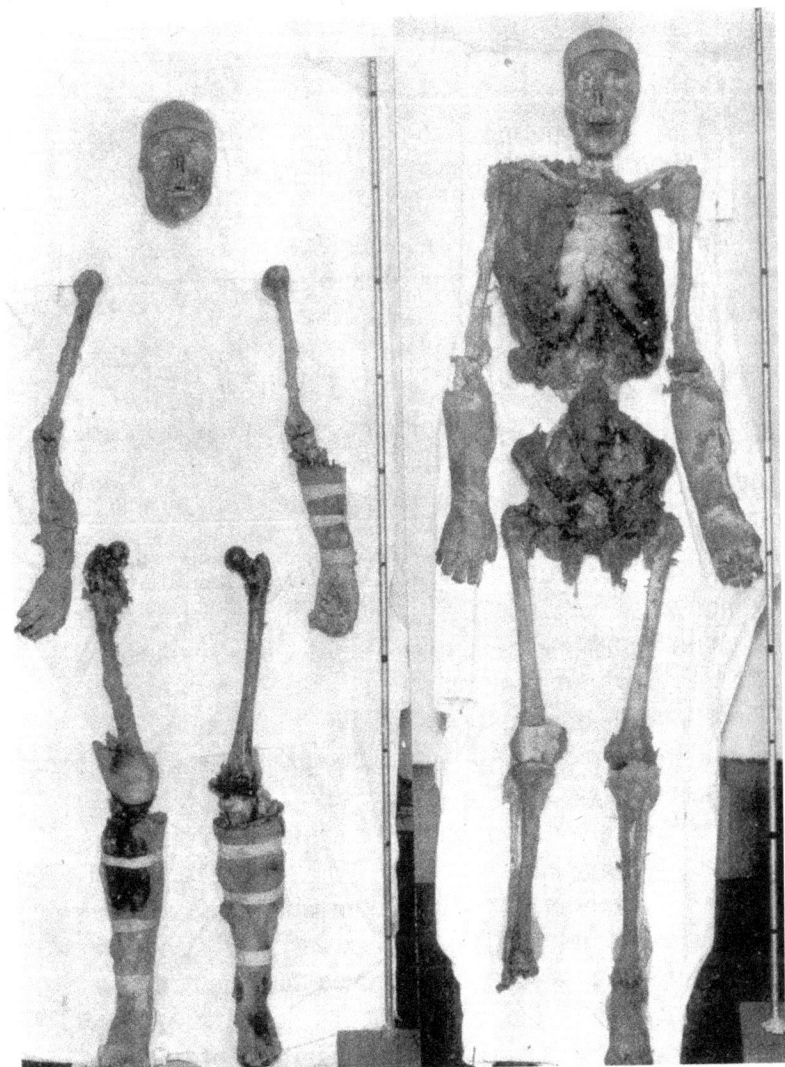

Body No 1 Body No 2
Source: Medico-Legal Aspects of the Ruxton Case, pg 61

As an integral part of the reconstruction process, it was crucial to establish the sex, age and stature of each of the two bodies.

Sex

The opinion as to the sex of Body No 1 was based on consideration of the soft parts attached to the skeleton, and of the general appearance of the skeleton itself. This was possible by examining the head and limbs only, since the trunk remained missing.

The features by which a skull is judged to be female are mainly negative. The skull retains the features of that of an adolescent person and does not display the heavier build and strong muscular attachments that develop in the male skull both at and after puberty.

The skull of Body No 1 was very lightly built and the same characteristics were displayed by all the main limb bones. They were short slender bones with ill-defined muscular markings.

All the results of the anatomical examination and measurements of the skeletal parts of Body No 1 consistently pointed to female sex. Therefore, there was no hesitation in drawing the conclusion that this body was female.

Body No 2 was also confirmed to be female because female sex organs were still present in the pelvis. Originally, it was believed that this body was that of a male, mainly because the skull and limb bones were of a heavier build than those of Body No 1. However, further detailed examination of the bones confirmed that the body was that of a female.

Body No 1

Observations of the parts available and especially the appearance of the face, despite mutilation, suggested that Body No 1 was that of a youngish woman. From a detailed examination of the epiphyseal ends of the limb-bones, of the sutures of the skull, and possibly the teeth, it was hoped to produce sufficient evidence to estimate the age within a narrow range.

Examination of the sutures (joints of the skull) revealed no sign of fusion or closure, which pointed to a strong probability that the age of the body was not over 30 years.

Taking the whole of the evidence, indications led to a probable age of between 20 and 22 years. A detailed examination of the teeth present in the jaws of Body No 1 centred on the eruption of the wisdom teeth. These do not usually appear before the 17th, but they are commonly erupted by the 21st to 24th years. It was estimated that the lower teeth indicated an age of 18 years and the upper teeth 20 years. Based on the calcification of the wisdom teeth, the approximate age of Skull No 1 was between 18 and 20 years.

Further examination of the epiphyseal ends of the limb bones of Body No 1 and their state of fusion, placed them within a range of between 18 and 25 years. All the available evidence led to the opinion that the most probable age lay between 20 and 21 years.

Body No 2

The estimate of the probable age of Body No 2 was based on observations similar to those made in respect of Body No 1. The complete union or fusion of the epiphysial end of the limb bones indicated a minimum age of 22 to 25 years.

Further examination of the skull of Body No 2 confirmed the general conclusion drawn from the examination of the limb bones but raised the minimum age to 30+ years.

The state of closure of the sutures of Skull No 2 was of particular value. Union of the bones was so advanced that there could be no doubt that the age was at least 30 years. Taken as a whole, the state of the sutures of the skull of No 2 Body justified the conclusion that the age lay between 30 and 55 years, whilst the balance of probability seemed to indicate that the ages lay more between 35 and 45 years.

Stature of the Bodies

When a body has been dismembered it may be possible to reconstruct it so that its whole length may be measured directly. Obviously, this depends to a large extent on whether all the parts of the body, including at least one of the lower limbs is available.

Body No 2 could be directly measured, but for Body No 1 the trunk was missing, so only indirect methods of measurement were possible. The formulae employed by the experts at Edinburgh were those devised by Karl Pearson, based on a mathematical study of measurements of limb bones and of statures of both male and female skeletons. The most reliable formulae were those that dealt with the measurements of four particular bones: the humerus, radius, femur and tibia.

Using Pearson's formulae, the living stature of

Mary Rogerson was estimated at between 4' 10" and 4' 11", whilst her actual known height was approximately 5' 0".

The probable living stature of Body No 2 of Isabella Ruxton lay between 4' 11" and 5' 1". The actual measurement of the reconstructed body was approximately 5' 3", while Mrs Ruxton's actual known height was 5'5".

In respect to the age and stature of Body No 1 and Body No 2, the conclusions of the medical experts corresponded closely to what was known of the missing women from Lancaster.

Mary Rogerson was 20 years of age whilst the estimated age of Body No 1 based on anatomical grounds was put at between 21 and 22 years. Dental analysis put the age at approximately 20 years and her stature was placed at approximately 5 feet in height. The estimated height from measurements of the limb-bones, was put at between 4'10" and 4' 11". Body No 2 Mrs Ruxton was 34 years of age whilst the estimated age was placed at between 35 and 45 years. Her living stature was approximately 5' 5" whilst the estimated height was placed at 5' 3".

Early in the examination, it had been observed that Head No 1 and Head Number 2 were very different in both size and shape. Known photographic portraits of the two missing Lancaster women indicated that Head No 1 could not be that of Mrs Ruxton and Head No 2 that of Mary Rogerson.

Professor James Brash did something that had never been attempted before in a criminal investigation in an attempt to achieve positive identification of the two victims. Two photographs of each of the women were used - a studio portrait of Mrs Ruxton and a photograph of Mary Rogerson. The two cleaned skulls were each photographed matching as closely as possible the positions of the heads in the photographs. The photographs were enlarged to the size of the skulls and shapes and features were traced in ink on transparent paper. Subsequent superimposition revealed that the portrait of Mrs Ruxton fitted the outline of Skull No 2 very well and similarly the picture of Mary Rogerson was found to fit over Skull No 1.

Portrait of Mrs Ruxton

Skull of Mrs Ruxton. Skull Negative on Portrait of Mrs Ruxton
Source: Detroit Free Press

Cause and Time of Death

The final objective of the medical examinations carried out by the experts at Edinburgh University on the remains, was to establish the cause and probable time of death of each body.

In respect of Body No 1 (Mary Rogerson), in the absence of the trunk, with its organs and of the tissue of the neck, it was not possible to define the cause of death. However, the bruises on the face and arms showed that violence had been applied shortly before death. There was also evidence that the bruise of the tongue had been produced probably an hour or two before death. The swelling of the tongue might have resulted from asphyxia, by violence or from the process of decomposition.

The injuries found on Body No 1 consisted of a lacerated and incised wound of the scalp, two small fractures of the skull and bruising of the tongue and both upper arms. However, it was not possible to define the cause of death in respect of Body No 1.

In respect of Body No 2, the congested state of the brain and lungs, and the presence of petechial haemorrhages on the surface of the lungs, suggested that the probable cause of death was asphyxia. The condition of the hyoid bone suggested that the neck had been forcibly compressed, and that the cause of death was manual strangulation. The tongue was in the condition commonly found after strangulation, and the pressure marks on it corresponded to the empty sockets of the teeth removed after death.

Identification of the Maggots

Dr Alexander G Mearns of the Institute of Hygiene at the University of Glasgow undertook the investigation of the maggots that infested the remains. He concluded that the only larvae possible were those of the Musca domestica or Common Blue-bottle. Dr Mearns explained that the total life span of the largest larvae taken from the remains could not have exceeded 12 days and was probably less. It was considered very unlikely that the eggs had been laid more than a day or two after the remains had been deposited in the ravine. The stage of development of the larvae was compatible with the remains having been deposited in the ravine about 12 to 14 days before their examination on 1st October 1935.

The result of this line of investigation not only corroborated the opinions expressed on other grounds, but also fitted the hypothesis that the remains had probably been deposited in the ravine during the early hours of the morning of Monday 16th September 1935.

Final Medical Summary

The neat dismemberment of the bodies without the use of a saw, and with very little damage to the joints, clearly implied possession of some anatomical knowledge. The removal of identifying features and of parts that might have suggested the cause of death, combined with the evidence of anatomical knowledge and of some skill in the extraction of teeth, presented a picture that fully supported the hypothesis that the person concerned was able to bring more than lay knowledge to bear on the task of dismemberment.

The question of the time required for cutting up the bodies and reducing them to the state in which they were found was of significance. The police contention was that Ruxton had the opportunity and time enough to do the work unobserved in his own home before the latest hour by which he must have begun his journey to Moffat on the Sunday night, the 15th/16th September.

Professor Glaister gave the opinion that the disarticulation and mutilation of Body No 2, including the removal of the abdominal organs and of the flesh from the bones, would probably have taken about 5 hours to complete. This was assuming that the operator had proper light and sharp instruments and possessed some dexterity.

However, the time required to disarticulate and mutilate Body No 1 would be considerably less since there was much less mutilation involved, and so was more likely to have been completed in 3 hours. It was maintained by the police that the remains had been deposited during the night of 15th/16th September and that the last consignment had been removed from 2 Dalton Square, Lancaster on Thursday 19th September. It was later established that

Ruxton had been to Moffat in the past and he knew the road there very well.

Ruxton's Interview and Arrest

At approximately 9:30 pm on Saturday 12th October 1935, Buck Ruxton arrived at the Chief Constable's Office for an arranged interview regarding the missing women from Lancaster. A number of police officers were in attendance, including some from Scotland, and the interview lasted throughout the night.

When requested to account for his movements between the 14th and 19th September, Ruxton produced a document which he had entitled 'My Movements' which he handed to the investigators before making a 'voluntary' statement. During the interview Ruxton denied that he had ever been to Scotland, yet he was unable to explain why his car registration number had been logged by a young cyclist who he had knocked off his bicycle in Kendal on the 17th September.

The Lancaster Police suggested to him that this incident was circumstantial evidence of an offence that had occurred when he was driving back to Lancaster after visiting Moffat. He was unable to explain why a police search of his house had revealed extensive traces of blood stains on the stairs, railings, balustrade and various carpets. This was despite evidence that the house had been thoroughly cleaned, and that several walls around the staircase had been recently re-decorated. He was also unable to explain why traces of human flesh and body tissue had been discovered within the drains of the property, particularly in the section of drains leading directly from the bathroom.

Throughout the several hours of the interview

with Ruxton, Lancaster Police conversed with their Scottish colleagues who had previously visited Ruxton's home to remove objects such as sections of wallpaper, carpeting and silverware for detailed forensic examination.

In the early hours of Sunday 13th October 1935, news came through to Lancaster Police that the finger and palm prints on the second set of human hands discovered with the remains were found to be a complete match for impressions on items from Dalton Square which Mary Jane Rogerson had handled.

This latest news sealed Ruxton's fate and at precisely 7:20 am on Sunday 13th October 1935 he was formally charged with the murder of Mary Rogerson.

The Forensic Investigation

One of the many incriminating facts in the Ruxton Case was the presence of numerous blood stains in the house at 2 Dalton Square. Proving that these stains were made by human blood involved many separate tests. However, there were in Ruxton's home so many stains that appeared to be blood, that it was virtually impossible to test them all in situ.

Consequently, certain parts of the stairs and most of the fixtures and fittings in the bathroom were removed by Lancaster Borough Police and sent to the Department of Forensic Medicine at Glasgow University for analysis. Accompanying these were the pieces of carpet, the stair pads and the suit given by Ruxton to his patient, Mrs Mary Hampshire, that the police had recovered from her.

The question of the age of the blood stains on several of the exhibits were given particular attention. At trial, Professor Glaister, when questioned by the defence counsel, stated that it was likely that the blood of the stair carpets was not very old. However, at the time of the trial, there was no reliable method of estimating accurately the age of the blood stains, which provided the defence with an advantage, if only temporarily. The saturation of certain parts of the stair carpet was revealed by the presence of blood clots.

The finding of human protein inside several of the stair rod holders strongly suggested that blood had been present on those stairs at one time. These factors served as an indication that the amount of blood originally present on the top flight of stairs must have been very considerable.

The quantity of blood found in the bathroom was not large, but in view of the evidence that certain parts of that room, the floor, the top of the built-in seat and the bath itself, had been washed, and in view of the wide distribution of the stains, this suggested that the amount of blood originally present had been considerably greater.

The hypothesis of the prosecution was that both women met with violent deaths at Dalton Square, Mrs Ruxton first, and then Mary Rogerson because she was the only witness to the murder of her mistress.

It was further suggested that both bodies had been dismembered in the bathroom and drained of blood in the bath itself. Ruxton's injured right hand might have been responsible for the blood stains on the bannister provided that when coming downstairs he had held his hand above the level of the top rail. It is hardly to be expected that a doctor with such injury would have refrained from taking some steps to control the flow of blood. In any case, such injury could not account for the condition of the carpets or the bath. No stains on the carpets had been seen by the domestic workers employed at Dalton Square before the disappearance of Mrs Ruxton and Mary Rogerson. The conclusions reached were that the hypothesis of the prosecution was quite consistent with all the evidence concerning the blood stains. The blood stains on the top staircase were compatible with considerable haemorrhage from serious bodily injury to one or both of the women.

Following his appearance at Lancaster Magistrates Court, Ruxton was remanded in custody. These were weekly remands from that date until 5th November when he was further charged with the murder of his common-law wife, Isabella.

By this date, the medical team at Edinburgh University had positively identified the remains of Body No 2 as that of Isabella Ruxton.

Following this second charge, Ruxton was further remanded from week to week on the application of the Director of Public Prosecutions. On 26th November, Ruxton's Committal Hearing was held at Lancaster Magistrates Court when all the evidence, both from the police investigation and the medical enquiry was presented.

This hearing lasted from the 26th of November until 13th December, when Ruxton was committed for trial at the Manchester Assizes on both charges. Evidence concerning the death of Mary Rogerson was admitted at the trial, although Ruxton was not being tried on the count charging him with her murder. It was held that such evidence tended to prove the killing of Mrs Ruxton, and was particularly relevant to the question of identification of the remains.

The strength of the case for the Prosecution was largely dependent upon the identification of the bodies. In law it was not necessary that there should be a body in order that a charge of murder may be presented against some person or persons. However, Article 768 of Section 9 of Halsbury's Laws of England states: 'Where one body or part of a body has been found, which is proved to be that of the person alleged to have been killed, the accused person should not be convicted either of murder or manslaughter, unless there is evidence either of the killing or of the death of the person alleged to have been killed. In the absence of such evidence there is no onus upon the accused to account for the disappearance or non-production of the person alleged to be killed'.

It follows from this ruling that Ruxton would not be convicted unless it could be proved 'beyond reasonable doubt' that the bodies found at Moffat were indeed those of Mrs Ruxton and Mary Rogerson. When the news of the disappearance of Isabella Ruxton and Mary Rogerson was communicated to Edinburgh together with their descriptions, it was possible to build convincing comparisons with Body No 1 and Body No 2 (Tables 1 and 2 on the following pages).

TABLE 1 Mary Jane Rogerson Body No 1 - Female Source: Medico-Legal Aspects of the Ruxton Case, Glaister and Brash (1937) page 108

Age	Twenty years (8th October, 1935).	Certainly between 18 and 25. Probably between 20 and 21.
Stature	About 5 ft.	4 ft. 10 in. to 4 ft. 11½ in. (without shoes).
Hair	Light brown.	Hair from scalp and body light brown.
Eyes	Blue. "Glide" in one.	Removed.
Complexion	Light. Freckles on nose and cheeks.	Ears, nose, lips, and most of skin of face removed; complexion of remainder of skin consistent.
Teeth	Old extraction of six teeth, four of them named.	Old extraction or loss of eight teeth, including the four named (see Chapter VII).
Neck	Short neck.	Very small larynx very highly situated.
Tonsils	Subject to tonsillitis.	Microscopic evidence consistent with recurrent tonsillitis.
Vaccination Marks	Four on left upper arm.	Four on left upper arm.
Finger-nails	Maidservant.	Trimmed but not regularly manicured; scratches indicating some form of manual work.
Scars	1. Abdominal scar—appendix operation.	1. Trunk missing.
	2. Operation for septic thumb which had left a mark.	2. First segment of right thumb denuded of tissue; no scar on left thumb.
Identifying Peculiarity	Birth marks (red patches) on right forearm near elbow.	Skin and soft tissues removed from upper third of forearm, and lower two-thirds of front only.
Size and Shape of Feet	Left shoe as evidence.	Cast of left foot fitted shoe (see Chapter IX).
Form of Head and Face	Two photographs in different positions.	Outlines of photographs of skull in same positions fitted (see Chapter X).
Finger-prints	Numerous imprints from house at 2 Dalton Square (see Chapter VIII).	Positively identified as the finger-prints of both hands and palmar impressions of left hand.
Breasts	Age 20, unmarried.	Single breast, appearance and structure consistent.

TABLE 2
Source: Medico-Legal Aspects of the Ruxton Case – Glaister and Brash (1937), page 111

	ISABELLA RUXTON	BODY No. 2 – FEMALE
Age	34 years 7 months (3rd October, 1935).	Certainly between 30 and 55. Probably between 35 and 45.
Stature	5 ft. 5 in. to 5 ft. 6 in.	5 ft. 3½ in. (without shoes).
Hair	Soft texture, mid-brown with patch of grey slightly to right of top of head.	Scalp completely removed; a few adherent hairs light to medium brown. Eyelashes dark brown. Available body hair mid-brown.
Eyes	Deep-set; grey-blue.	Removed.
Complexion	Fair.	Ears, nose, lips, and skin of face removed.
Teeth	Denture replacing three named teeth in gap which would show during life; old extraction of one other named tooth.	Old extraction or loss of fifteen teeth, including the four named (see Chapter VII).
Fingers and Nails	Long fingers. Recognisable nails — bevelled, brittle, growing tight at corners, rounded at ends, regularly manicured.	Terminal segments of all fingers removed.
Legs and Ankles	Thick ankles. Legs of same thickness from knees to ankles.	Soft tissues removed from legs.
Left Foot	Inflamed bunion of left big toe.	Hallux valgus of left foot; tissues removed over metatarso-phalangeal joint down to bone and joint opened. X-rays showed exostosis of head of metatarsal.
Size and Shape of Feet	Left shoe as evidence.	Cast of left foot fitted shoe (see Chapter IX).
Nose	Bridge uneven.	Removed, but bone and cartilage arched (see Chapter X).
Form of Head and Face	High forehead, high cheekbones, rather long jaw. Two photographs in different positions.	Corresponding features. Outlines of photographs of skull in same positions fitted (see Chapter X).
Breasts	Pendulous breasts; three children.	Appearance and structure of pair of breasts consistent.
Uterus	Three children.	Separate uterus. Could not be assigned but structure

Chapter Three

Manchester Crown Court (Author Photograph)

The Trial

R V RUXTON
MANCHESTER ASSIZE COURT.
BEFORE MR JUSTICE SINGLETON

CHARGED WITH THE MURDER OF ISABELLA RUXTON.
PLEADED: NOT GUILTY.
PROSECUTING COUNSEL:
DEFENCE COUNSEL:
Mr Joseph Jackson KC.
Mr Norman Birkett KC.
Mr David Maxwell Fyfe KC.
Mr Philip Kershaw, KC.
Mr Hartley Shawcross.

On Monday 2nd March 1936, the trial of Dr Buck Ruxton opened at Manchester Assizes and lasted a total of eleven days.

The trial began before Mr Justice Singleton and an all-male jury. Ruxton was charged with the murder of Isabella Ruxton his common-law wife, and a second charge of murdering Mary Jane Rogerson was added to the indictment, but he stood trial on the first charge only, to which he pleaded Not Guilty.

From the outset of the trial, the prosecution maintained that there was a witness to the murder of Mrs Ruxton, Mary Rogerson, and this is why she too met her death at the hands of Ruxton.

According to the prosecution, Ruxton who was inflamed by jealousy and paranoia, had murdered the two women in the family home at 2 Dalton Square, Lancaster on Sunday 15th September 1935. He had then disposed of the dismembered remains in the Gardenholme Linn stream near Moffat in Dumfriesshire, Scotland.

Mr Joseph Jackson KC stated: 'It does not need much imagination to suggest what probably happened in that house. It is very probable that Mary Jane Rogerson was a witness to the killing of Mrs Ruxton, and that is the reason that she too met her death. You will hear that Mrs Ruxton had received before her death, violent blows in the face then she was strangled.

The suggestion of the prosecution is that her death and that of Mary, took place outside the bedrooms on the landing at the top of the staircase. The reason for this is that from that point down the staircase right into the bathroom, there are traces of enormous quantities of blood. It is further suggested that when Mrs Ruxton went up to bed, a violent quarrel took place and Ruxton strangled his wife, and since Mary caught him in the act she too was killed. Mary's skull was fractured and she had several blows on the top of her head. She was then killed by some other means, probably a knife'.

Ruxton's defence counsel, Norman Birkett KC based the defence case on the contention that the bodies had been misidentified and that the two bodies recovered from the ravine were not those of Isabella Ruxton and Mary Jane Rogerson. He claimed that they belonged to two other unknown individuals and maintained that the prosecution evidence presented to the jury was flawed.

Birkett and his assistant counsel, Philip Kershaw KC, contended that the bloodstains found upon the suit and carpets that Ruxton had given to his patient Mrs Hampshire, had been innocently accrued over the years Ruxton had operated his medical practice in Lancaster. It was patently clear that the case for the prosecution had involved the most detailed preparation. There were over two hundred exhibits, together with eighteen complete sets of photographs of the various parts of the recovered bodies comprising 130 photographs to each set, and each member of the jury was given a set. There was also a long stream of witnesses, professors, pathologists, policemen, charwomen and dustmen each giving evidence.

On the 9th day of the trial, the sole witness for the defence, Dr Buck Ruxton himself, was called to the witness box. Birkett began his examination-in-chief by asking Ruxton some general questions about the years from 1930 to 1935. Birkett opened by asking Ruxton, 'What do you yourself say about your relationship with Mrs Ruxton during those years?'

Ruxton replied 'We could not live with each other, and we could not live without each other'.

Asked if there had been any quarrels between him and his wife, Ruxton replied that there had been, but that they lasted a very short time.

When the evidence of a police witness, Inspector Thompson of the Lancaster Police Force, was put to him that he had said his wife was unfaithful and he would kill her, Ruxton replied that he did not exactly say the word 'kill', although he did admit that he had 'unfortunately' accused his wife of being unfaithful.

Concentrating on the night of Saturday 14th September, Birkett asked Ruxton what happened when Mrs Ruxton came home from her visit to Blackpool earlier that the evening. He stated that Isabella came into the house and asked him for the key to the garage to put the car away. After she had done this, she came back inside and went up to her own bedroom.

Birkett then addressed Ruxton. 'It is suggested by the prosecution that on the morning of Sunday 15th September after your wife had come back home you killed her.'

In reply, Ruxton claimed that 'It is a deliberate fantastic story'.

Birkett continued by saying 'It is also suggested that on that Sunday morning you also killed Mary Rogerson,' to which Ruxton replied 'It is absolute bunkum with a capital B. Why should I kill my poor Mary?'

What happened on the Sunday according to Ruxton was that at about 6:30 am Mrs Ruxton came into his room and suggested they went out for the day, as they had done often before on the spur of the moment. When he got up, he went to get the car and on return found his wife and Mary in the living room. He went up to his bedroom and waited, and while he was in the bathroom, Isabella came in to make up and asked if he minded if she went to Edinburgh instead. Ruxton remarked: 'I got a little bit annoyed at Isabella for making me get up early and then changing her mind at the last minute'.

Ruxton then told her she could go but not in the car. As she was leaving, Mrs Ruxton said that Mary was going with her. He saw them leave the house together between 9:15 and 9:30 am. He could not say whether they had taken anything with them by way of clothing.

It was while he was looking for something for the children's breakfast that he found a tin of peaches. He tried to open the tin with a tin opener, but the blade was bent. He injured his right hand trying to knock the blade straight and the wound bled profusely as he went up the stairs to the bathroom.

Ruxton then offered various explanations for the blood stains in the house.

As for the bedroom doors, it was always his custom to keep them locked. He was also in the habit of buying petrol in cans because he used it to burn rubbish and waste in the rear yard. The extra supply of petrol he bought for the car on the Sunday morning was because his wife had used the car on the Saturday for her visit to Blackpool.

When further questioned by Birkett on the suit of clothes he gave to Mrs Hampshire, he denied that he had ever told her to burn them. As for the foul smell in the house, he attributed this to the charwoman stripping the walls and washing off the glue used to affix the wallpaper.

In concluding his examination-in-chief, Birkett asked Ruxton: 'So far as Mrs Ruxton is concerned, did you do any violence of any kind to her on the morning of Sunday 15th September 1935?'

Ruxton replied, 'Never, never, Sir' and Birkett continued.

'If she was strangled, had you any part or lot in it?'

Ruxton replied, 'Sir, I have never done it'.

'With regard to Mary Rogerson, so far as she is concerned, did you do any violence to her?' Birkett asked.

Ruxton replied, 'Never, let alone do it. I never thought of it. She has always been a dear child to my heart'.

Birkett continued, 'If Mary Rogerson is dead, had you any part in bringing about her death?'

Ruxton replied, 'Certainly not, a most ridiculous thing to suggest'.

Concluding his examination-in-chief, Norman Birkett asked Ruxton, 'Apart from what you have told us about their departure on the morning of Sunday 15th September, 1935, do you know anything else about their disappearance?'

Ruxton replied, 'No , I don't'.

On the tenth day of the trial, Mr Joseph Jackson KC, leading for the prosecution, rose to begin his cross-examination of Ruxton.

Jackson: I understand Mary was very dear to your heart?
Ruxton: Yes.
Jackson: You say she was a very loyal girl?
Ruxton: Yes, I would stake my reputation on that.
Jackson: One that would never allow any harm to come to her mistress?
Ruxton: She was not primarily meant for Isabella, she was loyal to everybody.
Jackson: She was a girl who would have stood by her mistress and defended her if attacked?
Ruxton: Yes, I am quite sure.

Jackson: Why is she not standing by you today if she is still alive?
Ruxton: That is not a question I can answer.
Jackson: Do you think your wife was unfaithful to you?
Ruxton: Yes, it has been going on since 1932.
Jackson: You have for a considerable time thought your wife unfaithful?
Ruxton: She has done some silly things that would not have been done by sensible women.
Jackson: Where do you say Mrs Ruxton is today if she is not dead?
Ruxton: Isabella has done the trick often of going to Holland without a passport. If one can do that, there is no knowing where she may be.
Jackson: If I understand your story, you were in the bathroom when she finally left the house, and she tapped on the door and said, Well, we are off, dear.
Ruxton: Yes, quite friendly.
Jackson: Have you ever been able to find a single person who ever saw your wife and Mary Rogerson leave your house on that morning?
Ruxton: I myself and my solicitor have made inquiries.

    After a break in the proceedings, Mr Jackson resumed his cross-examination of Ruxton by asking him about Miss Winifred Roberts who called at his house about 9:00 am on the morning of Sunday September 15th.
Jackson: Miss Roberts delivered some newspapers and rang the doorbell three times and you opened the door a little way.
Ruxton: I don't recall that.
Jackson: She says you told her that Mary the maid is away in Scotland with your wife.
Ruxton: I don't recollect having told anything to

Miss Roberts. I don't think I saw her at all.
Jackson: She says you were agitated. What had you to be agitated about at nine o'clock in the morning?
Ruxton: Nine o'clock in the morning, it could not be because Isabella left after nine o'clock.
Jackson: She says you were very agitated. It could not be your wife leaving you that agitated you?
Ruxton: I am telling you that I have never seen Miss Roberts.
Jackson: May I suggest the reason why you took so long to answer the bell is that you were busy cutting up the bodies of your wife and Mary Rogerson.
Ruxton: May I respectfully suggest that three children were in the house with me at that time.

When Mr Jackson began to question Ruxton about the suit he had given to his patient, Mrs Hampshire, Ruxton replied that the blood on the clothes had accumulated over several years as the result of his work. However, Jackson pushed Ruxton on the point:

Jackson: But surely that suit was sent to the cleaners in August and returned on the 17th August perfectly clean?
Ruxton: Isabella does all the cleaning. I know nothing about it. I don't remember it.

At this point, Judge Singleton asked Ruxton; 'If you have a suit which goes away to be cleaned, don't you notice the difference when it comes back?'

Ruxton's reply was 'Yes, but I don't recollect this particular suit'.

Jackson said, 'If it was cleaned as I say, the whole of this blood had accumulated since August 17th'.

Mr Jackson then pointed to a portion of a sheet among the exhibits and asked Ruxton: 'If that is the sheet from your wife's bed, can you explain how it

got round those bodies at Moffat?' The only answer Ruxton was able to give to this 'deadly' question was; 'How could it be, Sir?'
Jackson: Did you at any time purport to give away or deal with any clothes of Mary Rogerson?
Ruxton: Never.
Jackson: Did you at any time do any act of violence to Mrs Ruxton or Mary?
Ruxton: No, God is my judge.
Jackson: Or did you make any journeys to dispose of the remains?
Ruxton: No.

The rest of the tenth day of the trial was occupied with the closing speeches of counsel to the jury.

Prosecution: Closing Speech to the Jury – Mr Joseph Jackson KC

'Were these bodies found in the ravine those of Isabella Ruxton and Mary Rogerson? Once you are satisfied with that, I suggest you can have little doubt as to how they met their deaths. To be precise, Dr Ruxton, after having killed his wife by strangling her and when the maid came to the door, hearing a noise, the one witness to the crime, she too lost her life. She lost it simply because of the devotion and protection she had for her mistress.'

Outlining the inconsistencies in the accounts Ruxton had given to numerous individuals as to the whereabouts of his wife and maid, Jackson reminded the jury of the eyewitness testimony delivered by numerous individuals. He then turned to Ruxton's exhaustive efforts to destroy evidence, and to pacify Mary Rogerson's parents as to their daughter's whereabouts in the weeks between the murders and his final arrest. As regards the actual motive for the murders, Jackson concluded by suggesting that they lay in Ruxton's obsessive jealousy and violent temperament.

Defence: Closing Speech to the Jury – Mr Norman Birkett KC

In his closing speech delivered on Friday 13th March 1936, Birkett began:

'It is the duty of the Crown to prove beyond all reasonable doubt, the guilt of the person who stands at the bar as Dr Ruxton stands today. Suspicion is not enough, doubt is not enough, the accusing finger is not enough, the imaginative reconstructions of my learned friend are not enough. Even if the bodies found in the ravine were those of Mrs Ruxton and Mary Rogerson, it did not prove the Crown's case, particularly if Dr Ruxton's statement that they had left the house was true. Though their bodies were found in the ravine, though of a certainty these were the bodies, it has not been proved in the case against the defendant.

The Crown must prove the fact of Murder. Some other hand might have caused their death. The case for the Crown was that on the morning of Sunday 15th September 1935, the defendant's house was one of murder. Yet into that house came Mrs Oxley, Mrs Hampshire and two other women day after day seeing the stairs, the wallpaper, the carpets, the yard, the petrol and the fire, and none of them thought at the time that there was a single suspicious circumstance. There are many features of this case which are mysterious, dark and seemingly unfathomable.'

Birkett emphasised that the idea that the

motive for Mrs Ruxton's death (Ruxton's suspicions of his wife's infidelity) were merely conjecture. While some of the testimony delivered had alluded to the possibility that the bodies may have been those of Ruxton's wife and maid, these conclusions had been drawn from circumstantial evidence which did not prove that Ruxton had killed them. Closing his defence address, Birkett emphasised that in any British murder trial, the burden of proof was not on the defence, but the Crown.

The Judge's Summing-Up to the Jury: Mr Justice Singleton

The judge began by telling the jury that in order to prove the case for the prosecution, it must be proved that Mrs Ruxton had been murdered, and that the prisoner committed it.

Unless the Crown proved these two facts the case would fall. The prosecution sought to prove that Mrs Ruxton was murdered, by evidence that she had not been seen since Saturday 14th September, 1935, by evidence that her body or parts of it were discovered at Gardenholme Linn, and by evidence of blood-stains and marks found in the home at 2 Dalton Square, Lancaster.

The prosecution further sought to prove that the prisoner committed the murder by evidence that he was the only adult person in the house on the night or day of the disappearance, by evidence of the different accounts he had given, and by evidence of blood stains on his clothing and items in the house.

Allied to both questions were the body of Mary Rogerson and her clothing. The charge on which the prisoner was tried related to Mrs Ruxton but both she and Mary Rogerson were said to have been in the house on the night of 14th September, 1935. The prisoner was said to have told several persons that they were away together.

If Mary Rogerson's remains were firmly identified and if some portions of her body were found in the same bundle as those of Mrs Ruxton, that would help in determining the identity of Mrs Ruxton's body.

Dealing with the evidence of the witnesses who called at Dalton Square on the Sunday morning, 15th September, the judge asked the jury if it was not peculiar that if the prisoner had cut his hand with a knife or tin-opener, that he should be spending Sunday morning pulling up stair carpets. Similarly, if a doctor had cut his hand, it would be thought that he would have been very careful to have it well-bandaged.

The judge then drew the jury's attention to the state of the house on the afternoon of Sunday 15th September. He asked the jury if they could think from what they had seen in the case, that the cut hand would have accounted for the blood on the carpets, the shirt and the towels? Even if it could, then what about the bath? What inference could be drawn from the evidence of that bath which had normally been clean but was then a very dirty yellow to within six inches from the top. Down the front of the bath there were blood stains as well.

What inference could they draw when dealing with the evidence of one of the charwomen who said that Dr Ruxton had asked her to strip the paper from the stair walls, but not to bother with the top landing, which he would do in his spare time? Yet, he had an injury to his right hand.

Coming to the question of the bodies, the

judge said that the thing to be borne in mind was that there were two women missing from 2 Dalton Square at the time when the remains were found in Scotland. The bodies had been examined and the evidence undisputed. They were the bodies of two females. One was about 4ft 11ins or 4ft 11½ins, not much removed from the known height of Mary Rogerson. The other was about 5ft 4ins or 5ft 5ins, not much removed from the known height of Mrs Ruxton.

As to the age; one of the bodies was said to be between 18 and 25, the other between 35 and 45, Mary Rogerson's age was 20 and Mrs Ruxton's age was just over 34, meaning the figures were not far wrong.

The judge considered that whoever it was that dealt with those bodies had done it in a most extraordinary way. The bodies had not only been disarticulated completely, but also almost every sign which would enable the one or other to be recognised had been removed.

The jury's attention was then drawn to the time it would take to complete the disarticulation. Assuming that Mrs Ruxton had left Blackpool at 11:30 pm on the Saturday night, she would have arrived back in Lancaster at around 12:30 am on the Sunday morning. Was it possible for the prisoner to do that which it was said he had done by 9:30 am or 10 am on the Sunday morning?

Assuming that it was Mrs Ruxton who had been killed first, then between 12:30 am and 9:30 am on the Sunday morning, there was an available period of 9 hours.

The medical witnesses had stated that they had considered how long it would have taken to reduce Body No 2 into the state in which it was found. The consensus was a minimum of 5 hours.

Evidence was also given that in cases of asphyxia (strangulation) the blood remains fluid longer by up to possibly 12 hours. That meant there was time for the disarticulation of the bodies to take place late on Saturday night and Sunday morning. Everything, so far as one could gather, corresponded with the two missing women from Lancaster, and there was no evidence produced to the contrary.

Counsel for the defence had questioned Mr Jackson's assertion that if they were satisfied that those remains in the ravine at Moffat had been proved to be the remains of Mrs Ruxton and Miss Rogerson, their task was complete.

The judge then asked the jury to consider that if the two women went away on the Sunday morning as the prisoner had said, why should he be accused of the murder simply because they were dead? If the two women did go away, could they conceive who else might have murdered them? They could not have been cut up very well in that ravine, could they? They had been treated, according to the evidence, by a person of some anatomical skill - the disarticulations would appear to indicate that.

If these two women had been murdered by someone else, could they see the reason for the removal of signs of death or possible means of identification?

One by one, Judge Singleton called for the exhibits to be brought into court. Blood-stained stair-pads, the front panel of the bath, the child's rompers and the blouse which had wrapped one of the heads of the victims. All of these exhibits were shown once more to the jury.

The judge reminded the jury that the prisoner must be given the benefit of any reasonable doubt that there might be in the case. He also emphasised every point which could possibly be interpreted as being in the prisoner's favour. He particularly directed the jury's attention to the discrepancies between the statements of the prisoner and those of the witnesses, to the condition of the stair-pads and suit, to the attempts made by the prisoner to persuade witnesses to make statements which were untrue. He particularly emphasised the absence of any communication from the missing women in the long interval which had elapsed since their disappearance, and to the fact that no medical witnesses had been called to refute the evidence of those appearing for the Crown.

In his reference to the medical witnesses, he spoke in the highest terms of the 'distinguished body of evidence' which had been put before them. He had never 'seen expert witnesses more careful and more eager not to strain a point against an accused person'.

The judge continued by remarking that he found it difficult to imagine greater care and greater skill being used than was used by the distinguished professors of Edinburgh and Glasgow Universities in putting together the remains, in their examinations and arriving at their conclusion. He then referred to the 'coincidences' if the jury considered that is what they were - of a copy of the limited 'slip' edition of *The Sunday Graphic* which had been delivered to 2 Dalton Square, Ruxton's home, being found with the bodies, and the identical fault which existed in the portion of sheet found with the remains, and the single sheet left on Mrs Ruxton's bed. Mr Justice Singleton concluded his summing-up to the jury by saying that if there was any doubt in the case, the prisoner must have the benefit of that doubt, but if there was none, their verdict must be equally clear, and justice must be carried out.

Having retired to consider their verdict, the jury returned after deliberating for just one hour. They returned a verdict of GUILTY against Ruxton. Consequently, Mr Justice Singleton sentenced Ruxton to death. The judge was then informed by defence counsel Norman Birkett KC that the defendant intended to appeal the verdict.

*Manchester Strangeways Prison
(Common Attribution Photograph)*

The Appeal and Execution

Norman Birkett KC, Ruxton's counsel, lodged an appeal on the ground that the judge had misdirected the jury. He claimed the judge had omitted to direct them sufficiently as to the evidence of witnesses regarding the clean condition of Ruxton's car after the suggested journey to Moffat, and also about the state of the weather at Moffat at the material time.

The appeal was heard in the Court of Criminal Appeal in London on Monday 27th April 1936, before the Lord Chief Justice, Lord Hewart, Mr Justice de Parq and Mr Justice Goddard.

Birkett's argument centred around the fact that the doctor's car was clean on Monday 16th September although it had been raining at Moffat. His argument was that it was impossible that the car could have been driven more than 200 miles across wet moorland roads in Scotland. If the jury was satisfied that the car did not travel to Moffat on the night of Sunday, 15th September, then the whole case for the Crown would fall.

Birkett remarked: 'There was not a spot of blood on the car. Isn't that a most remarkable thing? Is it not of outstanding importance to the case that the car which was to connect the murder at Dalton Square with the ravine, had no spot of blood on it, and that having travelled all those miles on such a night, there was no mud and no staining?'

Without calling on Counsel for the Crown, the Appeal Court dismissed the appeal after consulting for only a few minutes. The Lord Chief Justice, Lord Hewart declared: 'The evidence that the dismembered bodies were those of Mrs Ruxton and Mary Rogerson were really overwhelming. There is nothing in the Summing-Up that can be said to faintly resemble misdirection. The application is of a kind which the Court cannot grant'. The appeal was therefore dismissed.

A petition from Lancaster residents urged clemency for Ruxton, and it collected over 10,000 signatures. Despite this, Buck Ruxton was hanged at Strangeways Prison, Manchester on the morning of Tuesday 12th May 1936.

Prior to the hanging, Ruxton was housed in the condemned cell situated at the end of 'B' wing in the central area of the prison and was guarded around the clock. On the appointed day, Ruxton was hanged by Thomas Pierrepoint, assisted by Robert Wilson.

According to Form LPC4, Ruxton was 5' 7½" tall and weighed 137 lbs, so he was given a drop of 7' 11" which was a textbook hanging.

The police had to deal with a very large crowd of people who had gathered outside the prison to see the execution notices posted on the main gates.

On the following Sunday 17th May 1936, *The News of the World* published a signed confession by Ruxton in his own handwriting admitting to the killing of his wife and maim. It read: 'I killed Mrs Ruxton in a fit of temper because I thought she had been with a man. I was mad at the time. Mary Rogerson was present at the time. I had to kill her'.

It does appear that while Ruxton was in custody in Manchester, he was visited by a representative of *The News of the World*. Ruxton handed the representative a sealed envelope telling him to take great care of it. He told him: 'They have charged me with murder, and I in turn charge you to place the envelope in safety and security. On no account must it be opened until my death, if I am to die. If I am acquitted, and I think I must be, you will hand it back to me'.

Ruxton saw the representative again during the trial and told him that in the event of his death, the envelope should be handed unopened to the editor. This request was duly carried out on the same day that Ruxton was executed. This sealed confession was unique in that as far as it is known, never before had such a document been entrusted to a reporter by someone facing execution.

It is believed that Ruxton's estate received £3,000 for the confession, his total estate being valued at £4,765. As for Ruxton's three children, Elizabeth, Diane and William, they were said to have been brought up in an orphanage in Cheshire. This ends one of the most gruesome yet fascinating crimes of the 20th century, particularly remembered for the innovative forensic techniques used to identify the victims and the location of their murder.

> Lancaster.
> 14.10.35.
>
> I killed Mrs Ruxton in a fit of temper because I thought she had been with a man. I was Mad at the time. Mary Rogerson was present at the time. I had to Kill her.
>
> B Ruxton

Buck Ruxton's Confession from The News of the World, *Sunday 17th May 1936*

Chapter Four

An Overview of the Case

'If doctors do take the law into their own hands, the facts are only likely to emerge by chance, through the whisperings of suspicion or rarely through carelessness in the disposal of the dead body.'

So wrote Professor Keith Simpson, the forensic pathologist in his autobiography, *Forty Years of Murder*, published in 1983. One of the blunders often made by those who attempt to dispose of the bodies of murdered victims is to leave identifiable articles with the remains. In this respect, the Ruxton Case is a classic example; the child's rompers, the newspapers, the blouse and the torn bed sheet all played a major role in tracing the remains back to 2 Dalton Square.

One of the first challenges facing a murderer is what to do about the victim's body. Disposal of a body requires method and resourcefulness, the main purpose being to conceal or at least, to delay the discovery of the crime. To overcome the difficulty of moving and transporting a body, murderers readily incline towards dismemberment. Reducing the body to small portions allows remains to be parcelled up for easier disposal. Once the body has been reduced to a number of basic components, the remaining parts may be individually wrapped for final disposal.

Unless carefully thought out in advance, this usually involves the perpetrator grabbing whatever clothing, bedsheets or blankets that come to hand to make a parcel or bundle. Newspapers have proved to be a popular material for this purpose, even though they may well offer valuable clues to the place and date of the crime. This is precisely what happened in the Ruxton case, where Ruxton wrapped parts of his victims in a special edition of a Sunday newspaper which provided police with vital co-ordinates to his crimes.

The date of *The Sunday Graphic and Sunday News* found with the remains coincided with the date on which the two women had disappeared from Lancaster. The circulation of this particular edition was restricted to the Morecambe and Lancaster areas of Lancashire. Evidence showed that a copy of this paper had been delivered to 2 Dalton Square, Lancaster on the morning of Sunday 15th September 1935.

The initial police investigation into the case began in Dumfries, Scotland, following the discovery of the human remains at Gardenholme Linn near Moffat on Sunday 29th September 1935. The enquiry centred on looking at recent reports of missing persons in the immediate area. It was considered very unlikely that two persons associated in some way, could disappear without at least one other person being aware of the fact. To this end, the police concentrated their attention to reports of dual disappearances.

At the beginning of October 1935, both Mrs Ruxton and Mary Rogerson had been reported missing to the Lancaster Police, and by the 11th October, it had been confirmed by anatomical examination that the remains found at Moffat represented two female bodies. Following press reports of the discovery of the remains, many of the inhabitants of Lancaster, including Ruxton's own charladies and some of his patients, harboured suspicions that there may very well have been a connection between these newspaper reports and the subsequent disappearances of Isabella Ruxton and

Mary Rogerson.

Many of the mutilations found on the remains did assist the pathologists in their search for evidence. The manner of dismemberment without the use of a saw, clearly demonstrated that the person or persons responsible was skilled in the use surgical knives and possessed anatomical and medical knowledge. Ruxton, in removing all those parts of the bodies that may have been of use in identification, he had undoubtedly tried to destroy evidence of sex. However, with that carelessness which so often leads to the undoing of criminals, he had left among the masses of flesh, fat and skin, three female breasts and parts of sex organs which proved that there were at least two female victims.

Witnesses abounded in the Ruxton case, numerous people visited Dalton Square on the Sunday morning, the 15th September during which time Ruxton was busy dismembering the bodies. Several of the charladies recalled foul odours in the house and unexplained blood stains on the stairs and in the bathroom. Ruxton hired a car to dispose of the bodies and then collided with a cyclist outside Kendal on his way back from Moffat.

Ever since the disappearance on the 14th September of Mrs Ruxton and Mary Jane Rogerson, Ruxton had been careering round Lancaster like a man possessed. He had fabricated all manner of stories to explain the women's disappearance, but none were convincing. He had hounded the Lancaster Police with demands that they search his house to quash vicious rumours he was responsible for the killing of his wife and maid.

From information received from various sources, suspicion quickly fell on Ruxton. His conduct at various meetings with the police since the disappearance of his wife and maid, together with their own knowledge of his jealous and violent disposition, confirmed the police's suspicions.

It is quite possible that initially, the Lancaster Police viewed Ruxton as an unstable person. However, when the police finally took up Ruxton's offer to search his home, they found other incriminating evidence. Despite evidence of a lengthy and exhaustive clean-up, the police found numerous blood stains, and the drains revealed traces of human tissue.

During this search of Ruxton's house, the police retrieved personal diaries going back to the period from 1919 to 1934, but the diary for 1935 was (not unexpectedly) missing. One entry showed that on 4th February 1931, they had gone together by car to Edinburgh via Moffat. At the police interview before his arrest, Ruxton had asserted that he had never visited Scotland.

There are three cardinal requisites for murder; Why? How? and When? which can be translated into motive, method and opportunity.

The How? of murder is the method or means of carrying out the killing. The When? is choosing the right moment by creating the opportunity to carry out the murder. This can involve pre-meditation or planning or be the result of a sudden impulse. Therefore, some murders can be completely 'opportunistic'. Other murders committed in the 'heat of the moment' or provocation, may have little regard to 'opportunities' - they just happen.

In the Ruxton case there is evidence for pre-meditation in that on the Sunday morning 15th September, Ruxton's charlady Mrs Agnes Oxley was asked not to report for work on that day. This has been interpreted as ensuring that Ruxton would not be disturbed in his work of dismembering the bodies of Mrs Ruxton and Mary Rogerson.

One of the most important common denominators of murder is that the offender and the victim are known to each other. The legal test for murder is 'intention' defined in legal terms as the mens rea or 'guilty mind'. This is further defined as 'malice aforethought'.

Most murders are committed by people who would be regarded as 'normal and rational'. These are the sort of people who one would expect to make some risk assessment and plan when forming the intention to kill someone. Yet, how often do they? The murderer's aim is to fulfil the intention whilst at the same time to minimise the chance of getting caught.

However, at the crucial point when planning is called for, rational thinking is rapidly diminished, and events go into 'free-fall'. One particular group which would be expected to have some advantage over others are members of the medical profession. They have the knowledge and skills, and also have the means at their disposal, in theory at least. However, in practice, they turn out to be no better than others when it comes to committing murder. This is particularly so when they leave evidence of their 'professional' expertise as was the case with Ruxton.

As regards Ruxton's 'motive' in the killing of his common-law wife, it has been suggested that this was the result of his jealous and violent disposition. Ruxton's relationship with Isabella was both stormy and passionate; he was excessively jealous and suspicious. They quarrelled incessantly because he firmly believed that she was having relationships with other men. It was observed by one commentator of the case that the mere sight of her dancing or even speaking to another man threw Ruxton into incontrollable fury.

The episode shortly before her disappearance when Mrs Ruxton visited Edinburgh in the company of the Edmondson family displayed just how firmly the idea was embedded in Ruxton's mind, when he believed that Isabella and the young Edmondson had spent the night together.

Ruxton did admit that sometimes there was a sexual motive behind the arguments with both himself and Isabella. They experienced enhanced pleasure from intimacy as part of their 'making-up' routine.

From a psychological perspective, it has been argued by psychologists that jealousy plays a vital role in keeping a relationship healthy. The one fundamental and dramatic gender difference is that women are much more likely than men to try to invoke a bit of jealousy in their partner. Psychological research has shown that most men misinterpret what a woman's smile really means and make the mistaken assumption that it is a signal of sexual interest.

A significant majority of women use jealousy to test the depth of their relationship. It would appear that women who feel less desirable than their partners are prone to using jealousy as a way of correcting the imbalance.

The problem with this psychological reasoning is that if jealousy is encouraged in a person who is vulnerable to delusions and paranoia, and is of a violent personality, it can bring about very dangerous consequences. The unanswerable question remains; were Ruxton's suspicions of his wife's infidelity unfounded and nothing more than mere conjecture, or was it a ploy on the part of Isabella to re-kindle a flagging relationship? Unfortunately, we will never know the answer to this question.

In retrospect, Ruxton's invitation that Mrs Hampshire and her husband take away the stair carpets and suit was certainly a reckless oversight on his part. This particular evidence alone could have convicted him. Evidence of carpets soaked in blood, strange stains on the bath, and clothing stained with blood found in the back yard all contributed to Ruxton's eventual downfall.

All these items provided an observable trace of clues left at the scene of the crime. These were welded into a complete watertight case by the police and scientific experts. It was the unassailable scientific testimony that weighed so heavily against

MEDICO-LEGAL ASPECTS
OF THE
RUXTON CASE

BY

JOHN GLAISTER, M.D., D.Sc., Barrister-at-Law
Regius Professor of Forensic Medicine, University of Glasgow

AND

JAMES COUPER BRASH, M.A., M.D., F.R.C.S.Ed.
Professor of Anatomy, University of Edinburgh

With one hundred and seventy-two illustrations

EDINBURGH
E. & S. LIVINGSTONE
16 AND 17 TEVIOT PLACE
1937

Ruxton, together with the testimony of his own charladies. The most enlightening aspect of the Ruxton case was the information derived from superimposing a photographs of the skulls of Mrs Ruxton and Mary Rogerson on to photographs of the heads of the missing women. The results of this innovative technique revealed how every detail of the skulls fitted with the photographs of the living victims. It could be argued that there was no certainty about the identification by this comparative technique, but Professor Brash never claimed there was.

In addition, Professor Brash had flexible casts made of the feet of the two reconstructed bodies. These casts fitted accurately into the shoes of both of the missing women. Although even this could not be accepted as incontrovertible proof of identity, it was nevertheless one more link in the chain of circumstantial evidence.

The Ruxton Case stands alone. It is notable primarily because the extent and character of the mutilation of the two victims provided a problem of reconstruction which demanded for its solution anatomical work in detail not hitherto required in such cases. It is also notable because the purposive removal of identifying features suggested a novel comparison of skulls and portraits which, with other circumstantial evidence, helped to place identification beyond doubt. In addition, much work in different branches of forensic medicine and in other specialised fields was found to be necessary. Attention is drawn to the important part played by the errors and omissions of the perpetrator of the crime in building up the case against him.

Even today, the Ruxton case is the single most quoted murder discussed in modern forensic science.

The area around Gardenholme Linn in Dumfriesshire where Ruxton disposed of the dismembered body parts became known locally as 'Ruxton's Dump'.

Ruxton's house at 2 Dalton Square, Lancaster remained empty for decades following the trial. In the 1980s, it underwent internal renovation before being acquired by Lancaster City Council for offices. Since the crimes, the building has remained firmly 'non-residential'.

The bath which featured prominently in the investigation and trial was removed to Lancashire Constabulary Headquarters at Hutton, near Preston. It was adapted for use as a water-trough for the police mounted section. It is believed that Ruxton's three children Elizabeth, Diane and William were brought up in an orphanage in the Wirral area of Cheshire.

'In many respects the murderer's canvas is his crime scene on which he leaves his brush strokes, either by design or by default. We may be shocked, entertained or informed by what we read while knowing that in murder cases, the unbelievable is all too often true. To read about murder, is to open a door into the territory occupied by those who transgress the boundaries observed by civilised society.'

Bizarre Crimes: Incredible Real-Life Murders by Robin Odell (Constable and Robinson Ltd, London, 2010) pp xiv-xvi

Selected Bibliography

BLUNDELL, RH & WILSON, GH 'The Trial of Buck Ruxton': *Famous Trials 3*, James H Hodge (ed) (Penguin Books, Harmondsworth, 1950).

GLAISTER, J & BRASH, JC *Medico-Legal Aspects of the Ruxton Case* (Livingstone, Edinburgh, 1937).

GOODMAN, J (ed) *Medical Murders: Classic True Crime Stories* (BCA, London, 1992).

HARDWICK, M *Doctors on Trial* (Jenkins, London, 1961).

HYDE, HM *Norman Birkett: The Life of Lord Birkett of Ulverston* (Reprint Society, London, 1964).

LANE, B *The Encyclopaedia of Forensic Science*, (Headline Book Publishing Plc, London, 1993).

MAPLES, WR & BROWNING, M *Dead Men Do Tell Tales: The Strange and Fascinating Cases of a Forensic Anthropologist* (Arrow Books, London, 2002).

MARRINER, B *Forensic Clues to Murder* (Arrow Books, London, 1991).

ODELL, R *Bizarre Crimes: Incredible Real-Life Murders* (Constable and Robinson Ltd, London, 2010).

POTTER, TF *The Deadly Dr Ruxton: How They Caught A Lancashire Double Killer* (Carnegie Publishing, Preston, 1984).

SIMPSON, K *Forty Years of Murder* (Granada Publishing Ltd, St. Alban's, 1984).

SMITH, SA *Mostly Murder* (Guild Publishing, London, 1959).

WILSON, C *Murder in the 1930s* (Carroll and Graff, London, 1992).

WYNN, D *On Trial for Murder* (Pan Books, London, 1996).

Archive Sources
Forensic Medicine Archive Project: Royal College of Physicians of Edinburgh: Sydney A. Smith Collection: Buck Ruxton (1935-1936).
Ref: 12 (111-25/185.

Edinburgh University Library: Special Collections and Archives: R v Ruxton (1936)
Ref: GB/237 – E 91-13.

Forensic Medical Archive Project: University of Glasgow, Case File R v Ruxton (1936).
Ref: GUAFM. 2A/25.

'Gruesome Evidence at Ruxton Trial' in *Aberdeen Journal*, December 12th, 1935, Page 10.

'Trial of Dr Ruxton' in *Dundee Courier*, March 10th, 1936.

www.ingramcontent.com/pod-product-compliance
Lightning Source LLC
Chambersburg PA
CBHW070303220526
45465CB00004B/1720